DANCING WITH A COWBOY

by

Sara Lindsay Rath

*for Patricia Emerson,
with warm regards,*

Sara Rath

11/05/06

Published by The Wisconsin Academy of
Sciences, Arts and Letters
1922 University Avenue
Madison, Wisconsin 53705

Manufactured in the United States of America

By the same author...

Whatever Happened to Fats Domino, and other poems

The Cosmic Virgin

Remembering the Wilderness

Easy Going - Guide to Madison & Dane County

Pioneer Photographer; Wisconsin's H. H. Bennett

About Cows

For A.D.,
who shared the songs of whippoorwills
and still listens to my poems.

ACKNOWLEDGMENTS

Acknowledgment is gratefully made to the following
publications, in which some of the poems in this book first
appeared:

The Boston Review: "Horses"

Green Mountains Review: "Dancing With a Cowboy"
"The Apron"
"Secret"
"In The Wings"

The Great River Review: "Saturday Night/Sunday Morning"

The Contemporary Review: "Sideshow"
"Poison"
"Out of Breath, Out of Time"
"Walking the Dog"
"Rumblings"
"Marian's Zucchini Bread

Transactions, The Journal of The Wisconsin Academy of
Sciences, Arts and Letters: "Wildflowers for Dorothy"

"Carp in Love at 4 AM" appeared in the *Festival of the Lakes*
broadside, summer, 1986.

"Flag Day," "Souvenirs," and "Killing Frost" appeared in
the *Wisconsin Poetry Today* anthology, Wisconsin Academy of
Sciences, Arts and Letters, 1991.

~~~

I would like to express my gratitude to the Ucross Founda-
tion and The MacDowell Colony, for their gifts of solitude;
and to David Wojahn, Susan Mitchell, Jack Myers and Mark
Doty for their patience, encouragement and guidance.

THE ONLY CHILD LEFT

IN THE SHADOWS OF THE FOOTHILLS

INTRODUCTION

"Sara Rath is a terrific poet," a reviewer of *Dancing With a Cowboy* said when he recommended that The Wisconsin Academy of Sciences, Arts and Letters publish the collection. And when one reads this volume of her poetry, one quickly realizes what the reviewer meant. Sara Rath has become a significant contributor to American poetry, and *Dancing with a Cowboy* will enhance that reputation. The ideas and emotions found in these poems are subtle, powerful, and revealing; intensely personal, while at the same time the author seems to speak to each of us individually about our own joy and pain. It is an astonishing accomplishment.

What we see is a poet forging and defining herself in the voice of poems based on real life experiences. There is an early sense of place, of life in a small town that is seen as a microcosm of a larger picture. The expected influence of family, close friends, and children is present, and these things, when coupled with writing, have helped the author through unfamiliar and sometimes difficult territory. We are witness to the going of a life that has zigged and zagged here and there as "I keep trying to get it right." But as personal as these revelations might be, there is still that common emotion that we share while watching a father die ("Her Father's Daughter") or when we suddenly discover that we have defined our lives in terms of other people, when "I'll look down and everything I'm wearing/has belonged to someone else" ("Souvenirs").

Remarkably, in spite of the change and disillusionment, Rath's poems are composed of a language without edge, without that anger or self pity or resignation that detracts. We hear the searching to express the inner self that is sometimes still that small, inquisitive child, sometimes the woman trying to save her own life.

It has taken courage to ignore the small town censor's voice whispering "what will people think?" and write poems that divulge a personal life. But as Mark Doty said when he introduced Sara Rath at a recent reading of her poetry "Sara creates herself in the voice of these poems—vulnerable, desiring, tough-minded and generous at once, straightforward, sure, and above all <u>genuine</u>."

As the editor of *Transactions,* the journal of The Wisconsin Academy of Sciences, Arts and Letters, it has been a pleasure to publish *Dancing With A Cowboy.* I hope the satisfaction that comes from its reading will be as great as that which has gone into its making.

Carl N. Haywood

*"When a group of cowboys and cowgirls
get together to dance and have a bit of
fun, cowgirls make a sport of tearing
the tag off an unsuspecting guy's pants.
If she's particularly amorous, she uses
her teeth."*
> The Montana Broke Tracking Guide
> Montana Broke Jeans

*"The more people you are, the more facets
you have to reflect the light."*
> Alice Walker,
> on McNeil-Lehrer News Hour

"All life is six to four against."
> H. L. Mencken

"Life is a 3 - 2 pitch."
> Chicago Cubs sports announcer

THINGS NO LONGER MYSTERIES

Can't Help Falling in Love . . .

"Well it was long ago and it
was far away, and it was so much
better than it is today..."
    Meat Loaf
    "Paradise by the Dashboard Light"

Nights when I was unhappy or couldn't sleep
I'd see him again. I'd be tan and beautiful
and he'd catch his breath when I'd appear,
then clumsily, helplessly he'd draw me close,
covering my neck, my eyes, my lips with rough kisses

and finally we would make love — in wild abandon
at first, then lazily. It didn't matter
that the fantasy was a cliché. After all those years
of dreams he is still in the Sarasota phone book.
I've forgotten how he says my name,

his voice is the same, that slow Southern drawl.
I try to sound casual but if I'd lost my virginity
at sixteen it would have been with him
on a soft Florida night like this, fragrant
with orange blossoms. We held hands on the beach,

cruised city streets, read poetry in the back seat,
stole a hubcap for his mother's car, were saved
in a Saturday revival at his father's church
then French kissed in the driveway until four a.m.
My parents thought I was safe with the minister's son.

I'd wrapped myself in memories of his caresses
(and a scarf to hide the love-bite on my neck)
all the way back to Wisconsin. And though my father
stopped at Presley's Grocery in Tupelo, Mississippi
so I could buy a Hershey bar, I kept on crying.

Of course he remembers me, he'd called me once
in college; the next day he was sent to Viet Nam.
And after I was married I burned all his letters
feeling a flash of satisfaction as the airmail
envelopes charred and crumpled, destroying

"there's this other girl back home..."
He remembers me. Can we get together? No,
he sold his drums and gave up his band
a couple years ago, plus booze and drugs, he's been
born again, Praise Jesus, born again.

I say I'm sorry, I am leaving this evening, but
I'm not leaving or sorry. I am in a hurry.
I want him seventeen again and rebellious,
I want a Saturday night in spring, Elvis
on the radio and the promise of rumbling thunder;

I want the taste of cigarettes on our breath,
his lips exploring my face, whispers in my hair,
hands upon my blouse then warm, then gentle on
my breasts. I want that hot, that urgent fumbling,
the frightening anguish, want him to shove

inside me and push and push his way
while I hold on tight this time and I
won't let go because I want to
enjoy the fear that he might that he could
that he would and this time I will let him.

2

Horses

Hammer's father ran a pony ring
at county fairs and carnivals, so
he knew about things like that.
Big head too large for his body,
"like a sledge hammer," the boys teased,
he was shy, blushed and stammered
but he knew about making babies
and that gave him stature. "We make
babies for you and what do you do
for us," he baited me once, watching me
spin on the monkey bars. I baited him back
letting my skirt tent over my head but
I was frightened and told on him,
had to go to the principal's office.
Hammer, too. You'd think he would hate
me after that. In my fourth grade
Valentines I found a red satin heart
from Hammer. Perfumed. His huge red
face belied his printed "Guess Who."
When we were nine, Hammer invented
Horses. Behind the school,
by the big oaks near the railroad tracks
the whole class, all fifteen of us
played Horses at recess. The boys
stuffed corn husks in their zippers,
snorted like stallions and the girls
became young mares, hair flying
in manes, enjoying the chase,
our breathless chance to lure
the boy we each liked best.
As we grew older the game was mentioned
less and less and this summer
if someone whispers "Horses"
at our class reunion, there will be
a stiff and awkward silence

while graying men and women relive
our dark secret: wild mustangs
bucking and racing, slapping our thighs
to make galloping hooves until
the fillies are caught by whooping
boys who'll climb on our backs.
We'll carry them a few steps
whipped by green branches then
fall exhausted in the dust
struggle to get away, frightened
girls again. I remember
I ran like crazy when Hammer
galloped after me, afraid
of his toothy grin, the heat
of his fierce red blush;
in terror of his knowledge
of things no longer mysteries,
still forbidden,
no longer safe.

The Millpond

Mitten slipping from my friend's fierce grip
it's my turn to be snapped at the crack
of the whip, speed wildly across the ice
propelled at the tip of a moving wave

of sound and light and joy, Splendid Terror!
Our line snakes back and I'm shot
forward rushing wind, flying, defying
slick ice and flumes. At the Millpond

we prove ourselves, warn each other
keep away from the flumes or be sucked
in the dam where you'll die! Now I'm nearing
forbidden borders, tempting peril,

loving it. Then — slap — flat on my belly
slide on my face, skid to a dead stop so
swiftly I cannot breathe; in a tilt of time
I don't exist, can't pull in air or even squeeze

a feeble cry for help. Far off I hear
friends collapse in a heap of laughing bodies,
untangle silvery blades with a shout, regroup.
Thick bluegreen laced with ribbons trailing

white, the ice below my cheek thumps like thunder,
rises and falls. Just below my own
Karen's face blooms, bloodless;
palms splayed out against the underside

of thick greeny window, pushing up. She cannot
escape. She was with us here last year,
summer, too... We raced off the pier
to bomb cannonballs into screaming kids

then floated, lazy, in lukewarm depths.
I know the climb to the trembling board,
the promise of its edge; shoving off,
plunging, the cold neat slice, descent

to black pudding bottom, thrust of toes
bright ceiling, rising rush to surface.
Lungs explode in splash of breath, beating
the sly possibility you'll never come up for air.

Karen can't be here,
they dragged the Millpond in July
found her body near the flumes,
fingered the bruise on her temple where she hit

the raft one late afternoon she dove alone
and didn't come home for supper. I can move
my stiff legs now. Jinglebells on pompoms,
round yarn poodles we girls wind and tie

to the toes of our skates each year
sound silly. Nearby, "Are you hurt?"
Here's Joanie, warm breath streaming
in cold air, come to rescue me.

She takes one hand and pulls me up on
wobbly ankles. "Guess what, my dad says
he kissed Sonja Henie once." She's trying
to make me smile. I wish she'd go away.

"Who cares," I say and look back to see
if Karen's face has melted yet. Someone's
started a fire in a ragged stump that
juts from the Millpond and pulls us closer.

My Life as a Spy

Crouched beneath the front porch and peering
through latticework I watched people come and go
never suspecting I was hiding among skeletons
of dead sparrows. Passersby on the sidewalk

never saw me, either; I perched among branches
of the cedar tree, made a little peep
once in awhile to see if they'd wonder what
they'd heard, what kind of bird,

and didn't blow my cover, not even when
concertina music woke me in the night
in my bed alone on the second floor of the house
my great-grandfather built, listening to laughter

and singing, good times foreign to my quiet family.
I learned how to work silently in my pajamas
quickly removing the piece of insulating board
Daddy had installed over a door to separate

the part that had been the maid's quarters
now rented to the new grade school principal
and his bride; he had a polka band, too,
a minor celebrity with a Sunday radio program

on the Shawano station. There's not much you can see
through a keyhole but kneeling with my private eye
at that smallest of windows I could share
their lives with an addictive rush of fear

risking my discovery on both sides
of that wall. They entertained a lot,
sang and drank beer and one night
when there wasn't a party but I was bored

I saw him in his underwear walking toward me
but I couldn't see into any of the rooms,
just the hallway the rooms opened off from. And when
I'd be invited to visit there in evenings

along with my classmates to drink Pepsi
pop popcorn and sing along while he squeezed out
the old-time songs he recorded with his band
I'd glance at their side of the keyhole thinking

it was the perfect set-up. I never got caught,
not for spying. But I hated long division
and one night on his way upstairs for supper
he paused to say hello to Mother and to mention

I wasn't working up to my potential in arithmetic
and by the way did she and Daddy realize
how serious I was about Dick, perhaps it would be good
to break that up. So he got me afterall

and my life became a misery of storyproblems
after school, Dick got a crush on Judy
and the music that woke me after that
was just annoying Polack noise.

In Memory of Melvin

The time Harvey Rosneau shone
his flashlight through the windshield
of the Hudson at the Millpond
(and I was in the backseat with Melvin —

My God, I loved a *Melvin*)
our steamy kisses fogging up the glass,
I worried for awhile. The cop
peering through the fog also

worked at the post office (one of
the hazards of living in a small town,)
so it was touchy, my father went there
twice a day to get the mail. Melvin wasn't

the kind of guy you bring home
to meet your folks. But nothing happened.
Nothing happened, Melvin, and I want
to remember your long eyelashes and blue eyes,

Harley Davidson, black leather jacket,
my very own James Dean, even on probation
a rebel just because, up from Chicago
to live with your sister. I wouldn't touch a beer

but loved to neck and sure
did a lot of that though never
went all the way with you despite your claims
and that reminds me of another summer,

you stopped on a Sunday afternoon
to tell me you were getting married.
We drove out in the country, parked, this time
to talk. When you tried to hold me

I said I'd heard she wasn't really pregnant.
But what I really meant was why not me,
why had we never gone that far.
You married Gloria afterall, a girl I'd known

since first grade. Her father had been killed
in Iwo Jima or some place like that.
I didn't see you anymore after
that August afternoon and didn't think

of you until one day while warming a bottle
for a baby of my own, you were
a traffic fatality, a name on the news,
drove your milk truck into a telephone pole

at twenty-four leaving your wife with three kids.
You were great in the back seat, the best,
Melvin, but I have been haunted ever since
wondering if I told you about the times

Gloria came over after school in first grade
to listen to our Eddy Arnold record, the one
called "My Daddy is Only a Picture." I'd offered
to play it for her and then she begged me

to play it day after day after day until
my mother found out
and made me stop. She said
it wasn't nice to make her cry.

Secret

I'd gone rollerskating to the end of the sidewalk
and back just before supper but my little brother
stopped me when I went past the grade school, said
our paperboy wanted to show me something

so I turned and he caught me, a high school boy,
pulled me back behind the building,
stretched out the elastic of my corduroys, shoved
his big fist down into my underpants. I knew

it wasn't right, tried to push him away.
"What're you doing," I wanted to know, squirming,
but he wouldn't tell, just fought hard
to keep his hand there. "I found it,"

he said finally, poking a fat finger
inside a place I had never explored. I began
to lose my balance, my rollerskates slipped,
I had to hang onto his shirt. "This is it," he grunted

low in his throat as though it was a contest
and he'd won, then let me fall down on the concrete,
grabbed his bag of papers and ran off
between the monkey bars and the merry-go-round.

I yelled for my frightened brother who'd been
hiding around the corner and we raced
home to ask Mother what the paper boy was looking for
but she never really said, just

"Tell me again," brushing back my bangs
like she did when I was sick,
"Everything." And Daddy left, I'd never
seen him so mad, slamming the kitchen door.

Blue Waltz

I remember the fragrance of Blue Waltz perfume,
(the small heart-shaped bottle, pointed baby blue cap)
romantic and sweet with a hint of sadness.
Twenty-five cents at our small town dime store.

The heart-shaped bottle with its baby blue cap
in the 2nd aisle, near the powder puffs —
twenty-five cents. I was enticed by that dime store
and solemnly dabbed perfume behind my ears

In the 2nd aisle, near the powder puffs
closing my eyes and dreaming of love.
I solemnly dabbed it behind my ears
feeling grown-up and sophisticated.

Now, closing my eyes and dreaming of love,
I remember the fragrance of Blue Waltz perfume,
feel grown-up and sophisticated,
romantic and sweet, with a hint of sadness.

Old Wounds

Layers of lies and time have sealed a trace
of graphite in my finger, a small dark secret
held almost forever. Even if I didn't remember
the surge of my pencil's stab, the sharp hurt
and spurt of blood, the memory wouldn't go away.
Those eighth grade days still whisper

like the rush of his hot breath upon my neck, whispered
threats caught in patterns his eyes would trace
on our budding breasts. We'd cross our arms, move away,
blushing; all the girls in our class shared this secret.
Our graduation photo reflects our grim, hurt
faces, seated beside a teacher we all remember,

his necktie blue and gold, our school colors. I remember
riding in his car to basketball games, the whispered
choice of the cheerleader who'd sit next to him; hurt
feelings, endless miles spent squeezed at his side trace
my hatred of blue and gold to his gleeful, secret
"opportunity corners," swinging the car sharply away

to the left so I'd have to lean into him. He had a way,
a roguish way of smiling as he'd touch us. I remember
when my pencil slipped I tried to keep it a secret
but he must have heard me cry out, and he whispered
that he had a bandaid. There was even a trace
of gentleness as he wiped away my blood though it hurt

to let him hold my hand. I wonder if he felt hurt
sometimes because we were afraid and turned away
when he'd approach our desks. Could someone trace
a motive for his arm brushing over our breasts? I remember
feeling ashamed, myself, when my boyfriend whispered,
"Can't you see what he's doing?" as though I were a secret

partner. Last summer an aging teacher's sad, secret
game caught up with him. Thirty years after us he hurt
a blind student, fondled her. But she did not whisper
to friends of his assault, she screamed. He was taken away
by police, went to court, lost his job. I remember
we didn't know the words to use, back then, to trace

our secret screams. Who'd have believed us, anyway?
How many girls were hurt by this man, remember his need
for love. Sly whispers, old wounds leave lasting traces.

Debbie: My Life

By now my heart's been broken as many times
as a movie star's so we're still a lot alike;
that's what I would tell you if I were in line
with your fans. Browsing in this bookstore aisle

I catch your voice above the buzz of the crowd
and am washed off balance in a wave of remembering:
At thirteen, in that crumpled snapshot I'm blowing
a puffed-up bubble so big it hides my smile

while I lean against a '55 convertible trying hard
to match the "mischevious sparkle" in her eyes,
a picture that will say with more than words
how much I adore her. "Isn't she sweet,"

a voice behind me murmers. "We don't see
many movie stars in Boston." Didn't I buy
every movie magazine with her picture on the cover
in Sebald's Drug Store, tape her *Photoplay* face

next to my mirror and practice that perky glance?
Stay as sweet as you are, I wrote, hoping she would find
solace knowing even common people cared when
Liz stole Eddie away. "Come right around here, Dear,"

Debbie guides a 60'ish woman in a lumpy raincoat who
clutches a signed glossy with *Debbie: My Life,*
frames an arm behind her while a nervous friend
snaps the shutter. I smile, too, at the sweetness

of this gesture, at the deftness of this motion,
the economy of warmth. We must not touch our idols,
Madame Bovary advises, the gilt sticks to our fingers.
Just like DubbleBubble, Debbie:

I never mailed the letter or the snapshot,
not certain you wouldn't toss them aside. So
I won't get too close and even now
will not confess that

I pushed my father's workbenches together
in our dusty carriage barn and formed a stage
where I sang your songs and danced for
audiences of sparrows, frightened squirrels.

Carp in Love at 4 a.m.

Slipping awake in the silvered promise
of early hours, I hear fish
slap the surface of the lake

flip high in bursts of passion
splash deep toward greeny depths
rippling coalescent circles

against the silence of false dawn. I float
awhile then swiftly slide with glimmering
carp and plunge toward sleep again,

an underwater world of moss and dreams
where luminous sheets of pillowed algae
entice me to join the swim,

the halcyon glide. Beguiled
by spawning courtship I surrender
to an auroral dance, my body sleek

and fluid, swimming to amphibious songs.
We play in primitive orgy, weave around
around each other, my warm eggs

released before I rise and surface
to mirrored morning.
Now, dripping after shower I catch

a shimmered reflection, and
wonder at these watery eyes,
the slick glaze upon my face,

half-mooned gills curled on my neck
my shoulders shawled
with irridescent scales.

Flash

You saw me alright,
warm spring afternoon, you and your daughter
stretched out in the sun like greased seals,
all slippery. You told the police
I was stripped and standing naked at the base
of the Century Avenue Bridge. I heard you
tell the girl you thought I was fishing. Well,
I was holding a stiff rod. And I took off
after you went inside,
after I heard you laughing.
That's what I wanted, your reaction,

that's what I go for
so I always try to do it
in front of two or three at a time,
girls in their late 20's, early 30's,
like Lillian, a married gal
who seduced me once when I was a kid;
I was mowing her lawn. Seeing me
sweaty turned her on. Sure,
I get caught. Sometimes
I drive around with my pants down
but if I can do it in front of

some woman I don't know,
it's better. The last thing
I want to do is hurt anybody,
and the worst I've ever done is
beat off, I suppose. One time
some college girls said
you don't have to do this, come on,
have a drink. They told me
they'd watch me whenever I needed it
and they wouldn't call the cops.
I tried it for awhile

but it wasn't the same,
part of it's got to be the guilt,
I have to feel bad afterwards.
There's a school of thought that says
people like me oughta be locked up
until it hurts long enough
and hard enough and we won't do it
anymore. Well I lost my job,
my home, my wife, my kids,
and I still can't stop. How much pain
we talking about here, anyways?

Tap & Ballet

Sandy and I took dancing lessons Saturdays
in The Chatterbox, a cool hotel taproom
that smelled sour, of spilled beer, stale smoke.
Mother drove each week and Sandy went along.
I recall very little about her, except she attended

our Sunday School, wore glasses. It's her brown
eyes I remember most: they were wide and trusting
and, because I was older, she followed me around.
In our patent leather tap shoes we shuffled and slapped
the wooden floor, admiring ourselves and the girls

in the mirror, holding our arms out like wings.
When I looked down I could see my thighs wobble
and our teacher, a plain young woman eager
to instruct but rough around the edges said
"Dassn't" and "Youse girls," which made me suspect

her knowledge of dance and everything else. She claimed
it would be years before she'd let me dance on my toes,
that I'd have to practice with soft slippers until
my feet got stronger. So I said Goodbye, Ballet,
and Tap went, too. It was spring, maybe near Easter.

Sandy quit when I did; she needed the ride.
Then one Sunday in front of the congregation
in junior choir Sandy started to tremble. I saw her
shake and caught her eye before she fell forward
straight as a board, right onto the floor.

Men hurried up to carry her limp body outside,
lay her on the grass and loosen her dress, whispering
"move aside so she can breathe." We stood around
and watched Sandy wake pale and frightened. It was
like something had grabbed her by the throat,

pulled her down. I didn't want to get too close
after that, afraid of the spectacle she'd caused.
I was embarrassed, afraid. When she questioned me
with those warm brown eyes her thick-lensed glasses
made enormous, I felt guilty. And on a summer morning,

one Saturday when we could have been dancing,
Sandy's father backed his tractor and wagon
right over her. I couldn't go to the funeral
at our church, didn't want to see her lying there
white and silent as if she'd fainted.

And every time I thought about it (still can't
push the thought away), I wondered how such an awful
thing could have happened, what her father said
when he came in the house. If she'd have been
with me would Sandy be alive now and dancing

on her toes? Within the year her mother was
pregnant again. I watched her parents closely
from my seat in the choir each Sunday, hurt
and angry they wanted a new baby to take the place
of their only child. Would it wear her clothes?

Her dancing shoes someday? Would God
forgive me for quitting Tap and Ballet?

WAITING FOR DARKNESS

The Apron

Don't be afraid to remember this, Mother.
You were younger than I am now,
wearing an apron with a ruffled bib.
I'd come home to an empty house,
slanting afternoon sun a rainbow

through the bevelled diamonds of the dining room window
but your apron, the one you always wore
was missing from its hook near the kitchen door
so I felt you were nearby. I know
how important this is to you, Mother,

how the words I write down worry you,
but I remember the stench of wet feathers,
that stink that both drew me toward you
and shoved me away. You were sitting
in the shade of overgrown lilacs

on the concrete entrance to the carriage barn,
a pail of scalding water between your legs
and a steaming wet, headless chicken, half plucked,
hanging in your arms.
I must have asked what you were doing

although I could clearly see what you were doing,
undressing a chicken so it would be "dressed."
The contradiction amused me but your face
flushed with the effort should have been a warning.
You held the bird out for me to see,

held it upside down by its rubbery yellow feet
skin slippery as it emerged from the steam,
the dangling neck, sloppy, flopping wings,
you dunked it into the pail, and pulled
it back up again, dripping,

clenched an angry fistful of feathers and pulled
a soft feathery rip
stripping the matted mass from the orange
flesh and flinging it toward
the newspapers at your feet.

But the feathers stuck to your fist,
to your fingers, and you wore them on your forearms,
they were pasted on your cheek
wisped in your hair where it fell wet
on your forehead and the

tears I noticed later.
"Is it one of Grandpa's?" I asked, needing to
say something and you nodded. Mother,
I know better than to ask you again
why you burned your wedding dress,

or why you ran into your bedroom and slammed the door
night after night after night.
But the first time I really saw you crying
out in the backyard with that pitiful chicken
hanging from your outstretched arms

why couldn't I comfort you?
Or did I imagine the whole scene,
chicken, feathers, tears?
Do you recall a calico apron
soaked with watery blood?

Mrs. Pittie's Fire

I want to go back to that firey summer morning,
to the crowd of neighbors at the end of our street
watching the weatherbeaten house come crashing down
consumed by roaring tongues. Ashes drifted

onto our hair, brushed our pajamas, fragile gray
flakes fell on Mrs. Pittie. Then firemen
came out the front door with her rocking chair
and placed it in the yard so she could sit

and watch her house and possessions burn.
Charred timbers and flickering debris didn't
create much excitement after a couple hours
so we turned and walked back home, my mother and I

and the undertaker's wife in her shortie pajamas,
nightgowned women in pincurls, men in their underwear,
townspeople torn from their beds by the siren
that had sliced through the sunrise like a hot

orange ribbon. Impressed by disaster, I chose a doll
I was fond of to give to Mrs. Pittie's granddaughter
but I was ignored when I delivered it,
she was busy with other new toys and I

suppose I was näive to wish that anyone else
could love that doll like I did. Still,
I recall my disappointment, the way she set it aside.
My expectations always supercede the actual. If

I could go back to that morning in June
when I heard the flames, before I heard the siren,
before I heard my father go to the telephone
to ask where the fire was and not take the car;

if I could dab calamine lotion on my poison ivy,
see the sun rise over the Catholic church
gilding the cool mist that had settled on our village
overnight, then wake to the same absurd dream

with my neighbors; watch my father rescue
her sewing machine and her kitchen stepstool,
see a wicker flowerbox of red geraniums
fall to the ground with a soggy plunk, I would go

home after the fire and remember Christmas
caroling at Mrs. Pittie's, the sour smell
of kerosene and old breath that met us at the door.
Dried rose petals. A blue Milk of Magnesia bottle

on top of her radio holding a peacock feather
that bobbed in the wind while we sang "Silent Night."
I would not eat breakfast but would sit in the swing.
Smoke from the fire would move across the sky

in its own black cloud, and I'd try to imagine
how a peacock feather burned:
in one big whoosh. Or did it crinkle and melt?
I'd see it catch a spark in my mind

and for one moment, irridescent
blue green and gold would blend
in a brilliance of rippling flame before
it shriveled into a hollow, silvery curl.

Poison

I'd played for years along the edge of the pines
between our backyard and the woods but never
caught poison ivy before. The doctor said
it was an unusual case, so severe and yet

so self-contained. The tri-lobed leaves had been
a brilliant reddish-orange and gold that autumn,
the autumn Lana Miller came back to school with a
sprained wrist wrapped in a bandage, all our friends

stood around her in sixth grade like it was a big deal.
So I plucked a flaming leaf one afternoon just to see
if anything would happen, rubbed it on my arm
and then rubbed another, waiting for a rash to rise

from the pale flesh until finally small blisters formed.
But the doctor wouldn't give me a bandage, he said
it should be exposed to air. The burning pain
and thick weeping crust oozing with yellow pus

turned my classmates away in revulsion; no one
wanted to look, not even me. I smeared pink calamine
to cool the hot itch and after it spread to my legs
Mother put on gloves and a long sleeved shirt,

pulled up all the vines and burned them.
But she stood in the smoke from the bonfire
after dark, and when she awoke the next morning
her eyes were only narrow slits in a strangely

swollen, Asian mask. We had to lead her,
blind, from the car to the dermatologist.
The elevator operator looked at Mother
and cried. And we didn't even know her.

Wildflowers for Dorothy

That was the summer I waited for darkness,
and told myself I didn't have time.
I pretended to ignore my friend
who lived alone with her widowed father
and sold subscriptions to magazines.
She seemed as quaint and old-fashioned
as a childhood fantasy I'd outgrown.

Each May Day I'd searched
for the earliest hepaticas
wood-sorrel, buttercups, trillium,
yellow violets, wrapping a quaint
nosegay in a paper doily laced
with ribbon. I'd place it in Dorothy's lap
near her hand, a dead white bird
on the shawl concealing
her withered legs.

That summer I slipped books of Gothic romance
out of the village library and hid
in my bedroom to dream until twilight.
Later, Dick and I lay in the long wet grass
of the park behind the bandstand, pushing
adolescent bodies against each other
until our cheeks were chapped
and we were exhausted, breathless, from
silent passion in the streetlights' shadows.

The papery-thin whiteness of the dead
bird hand Dorothy waved in my dreams
was a haunting farewell.
That summer wood-sorrel and rue anemone
wilted in a jelly jar next to my bed.
I pressed violets between pages
of Teasdale's poems, plucked petals
from bloodroots and recited the frightening
litany he loves me, he loves me
not, he loves me...

My Sister's Wedding: A Snapshot

If you could hear the thunder, or see the purpling
cumulus crouching off to the side; if you knew
this was a rusty houseboat still tied to the pier
or could feel the rain (that's not just a white mist
out there on the water); if you could have heard
my mother's warning when I arrived to please
not spoil my sister's wedding by making a fuss

over a little storm, you might understand my cynical smile.
Or maybe I am remembering it was my idea, her
getting married on a houseboat, certain it would be
much simpler, less chaotic than walking down the aisle
of our small church up north, buzzing in my ears
and bubbles in my vision. But I am certain
my suggestion meant the Mississippi River,

too far away for everyone to come. So here we are
on Lake Mendota, still within the city limits.
And we're all in the picture, even Mother's favorite
minister from back home, he's the one robed in black,
his back to the camera, holding the yellow-highlighted
typescript; a year later he will fall into
the clown ministry, dress in ruffles and polkadots,

wear a bulbous red nose to test his congregation.
My brother and I felt he'd already taken a giant leap
in that direction; I can see that secret knowledge
on my brother's face, he's standing next to Mother
who is nervously smiling at the floor of the boat,
probably wondering when I'll bolt and run for cover.
There's no evidence, either, of the wedding dinner

at the Edgewater later that afternoon or the reverend,
tipsy by then from champagne and seated at the bar
who will grab me, trap me within his chunky thighs
while reaching for another drink as I struggle
to get away, anxious to switch placecards so the matron
of honor won't be seated next to him; there's no
trace of the rosepetal trail my brother followed

after the blessing, a battered boutonniere that led
to the men's room, the minister bowing and stripes of vomit
down the reverend trousers. And there isn't a clue
of the evening cruise or the sheriff's boat that stopped us
to warn of another storm approaching and hand a ticket
over the side because our running lights were out.
No, I didn't make waves. You can see how I'm struggling

not to spoil this solemn occasion, part of the self-
conscious circle around my happy sister
and her new husband; the ones in the center
wearing red roses, they seem serene. All this fuss
for less than five years of marriage. Across from
the woman in violet with a lavender rinse
in her hair, I am the only one wearing a hat.

Sideshow

*"Olga, the bearded lady yearned
to be a stenographer and kept
geraniums on her windowill..."*
Diane Arbus

Whenever Ludmilla tells me the story
I am holding onto her hand and wandering
wide-eyed down the midway in hot August sun.
And when the wind snaps canvas posters,

turning our heads toward Baby Sally
The World's Fattest Woman, The Alligator Man
and The Children of Sin, yes, I'll pretend
to hand over the sticky nickel in my palm

and we'll enter the tent where two
monkeylike creatures cursed by the incest
of their parents, sit in highchairs,
dressed like children but with crepy skin

and dog collars around their necks
chaining them together. I will be at home
with the freaks — bearded ladies, Siamese twins,
midgets, giants, living skeletons —

people who have to sidestep their desire
for approval instead of forgiveness.
The canvas tent is stuffy; we are pushed
off to the edge by the anxious crowd,

near the side where the monkey/girl is seated
looking out at the curious. When her eyes
catch ours she smiles with a childlike joy
of recognition and we wave back. But the barker

jerks on her chain and she slaps at him as
people mock and jeer. I've heard it before, that
laughter: last winter I sat here on the edge
of the lake watching Christmas lights

around the shore reflect a festive necklace
of rubies and emeralds in black ice.
Dogs barked far away and a woman
in the distance shrieked with happiness

that tore at my throat like a jagged collar.
I don't think I would have to peroxide
my hair, get a skull tattooed on my bicep
to parade on the State Fair Midway. Could I

travel with the sideshow as one of the *extremes*?
After Ludmilla saw them she returned at night
discovered where they lived, a box-like bed
behind a fence, half-eaten food, clusters of flies.

The woman/girl reached out to her with a wizened hand
to beg her please, help them escape. But my friend
was caught and chased away; I think that's the part
I like best about her story, when she wanted

to help but there was nothing she could do.
Running away is never the answer; where
would we hide? This summer
never ends. It's the hottest in memory.

In a Sentimental Mood

You pull your shirt over your head and set it aside
while I find the sheet with the pink rosebuds.
And if you're thoughtful, if you remember,
you will bring the comb and scissors

down to the kitchen where I've placed the chair
under the light. You sit and I swirl the sheet
around your shoulders; usually we're listening
to the Big Band Show on JOY-107

because it's Sunday, and I fasten the rosebud cape
behind your neck with an old diaper pin. A mellow voice
is advertising a nursing home as I begin to barber.
I can see the pink delicacy of your skull

through the thinning wisps and try to tease you
out of your morning gloom. It's time for
"Mystery Discs," this week it's girl singers
so I ignore your indifference

and try to guess *Who's Sorry Now*
while I begin with eyebrows
white and shaggy, one wider than the other
and tufts of hair that spray

out at odd angles. After eyebrows
I start on sideburns, fit the comb
between your ear and temple and trim,
letting the traces sprinkle

into the crease of my elbow, sometimes
to the floor. One sideburn, then the other,
a challenge to get them to match.
Doris Day. Much younger, though and now

I guess an early Ella just to make you snort,
I know I'm wrong; it's not my era,
anything to keep up the chatter.
"Are you almost done?"

Your first words and you know
I'm far from it, working around that vulnerable
curve where your jaw hinges just below your ear,
the flesh tender, baby white, pulsing with your heartbeat.

I take a deep breath
but go for the nape of your neck,
use your razor to scrape the fuzz
and by the time I begin your beard

you are glowering and shift with impatience.
I muster self-control, shake the ache from my hand,
Ain't Nobody's Business if I Do, right, Billie? You
stare straight ahead. I part your long legs

to stand between and shape the slope
of your beard to your jaw in short,
sharp snips. Mustache: thin a bit then cut
straight across the upper lip. A quick kiss

to surprise you, then undo the pin as you stand up
and walk away brushing off bristly hair.
"You're welcome," I shout while reaching for the broom
and dustpan. I'll shake the sheet outdoors.

In the Wings

Flashbulbs are popping and I am scratching bites
waiting for Dad to get done talking with the senator
who will save us from Mother's wilderness. And
in the clipping in the scrapbook

she will keep for me I can see the photograph
taken the night we gave the deed for Grandpa's land
to the city for a new athletic park,
June 17, 1951: my father and the two men

who'd signed Joe's diploma and Joe
looking out over the podium he pounded hard
an hour ago up on this plywood stage saying
he'd hunted skunks back on his farm when he was a boy

and anybody who has to do that disagreeable job stands
a good chance of getting contaminated by the smell.
Joe and my father were pals, or so my Daddy brags,
and the truth is there's a plaque near the entrance

of the gym at Little Wolf High School that lists
our distinguished graduates. One of them
is Senator Joseph R. McCarthy, Class of '28
same as my dad. Mother says when the Russians come

we'll run away to our cabin at Mercer
and live on fish and berries. Digging up Reds
in Washington is just like hunting skunks, Joe says.
"He and I used to rassle together after school

down in the woods," Daddy tells me again with pride
when he finally takes my hand to walk home,
"He's a smart man, don't ever kid yourself about that."
Here in the new park next to Grandpa's woods

I can hear the Little Wolf River
over there along the shadows
where the bright new lights
run out to meet the dark,

lights that bedazzle the moths
and the mosquitoes and the modest crowd
of townspeople and farmers, all friends of our family
here to witness the homecoming.

Her Father's Daughter

He cannot hear my urgent whisper
to give up, please die. We've had
seven days of deathwatch, Daddy:
I barely recognize this remnant
of the man who fathered me —
eighty pounds, few teeth, curled
like a bald baby into grotesque
fetal curve after so many years
of struggle. He was never
such a fighter in his life.

~ ~ ~

I am four. In a yellow dress
with bows in my hair, standing
in thin wintry sunshine on snowcovered steps.
Mother says pretend I'm whistling for Daddy
to come home for dinner. I do that
every day, he says he always hears me,
arrives by the time the town fire siren
says it's noon. Now he's walking
toward me, hands in overcoat pockets,
his shadow almost up to my head
while Mother shivers in her apron,
aims her camera. My baby brother
is asleep inside the house and my sister
won't be born for years. But
I've looked aside, blurring my face...

Above my shoulder a small wooden box
with hinged door is fastened
to the porch. It has a tablet inside,
a pencil on a string. *Daddy,* I would
write my secret message if I could, *Guess
who will be the last one of us you will see.*
Hi, Honey... you will say just as you are
greeting me now and I will pretend
there is a flicker of recognition
behind the blank gaze of your hazel eyes
as though you know who I am
and love me anyway.

~ ~ ~

I will not cry when I try
to close his eyes tonight;
not as much as I cried when he spanked me
with the ping-pong paddle for talking back,
or when he said my new brassiere made
my breasts stick out too far, or
when he stayed up past midnight
to call me a whore for sneaking away
to be with Dick, a Catholic boy
he knew I loved to kiss.

The day he sold the lumberyard
I watched my father come in from the car
with a guarded glance and crumple
in the kitchen where Mother
soothed him in an unfamiliar voice.
I hid in my room to weep for Grandpa,
for wooden kegs of two-penny nails,
wallpaper books and days of climbing
stairs of lumber to warehouse eaves
inhaling the pitch and pine of forests.
He moved us to Florida and back again,
tried Irish sweepstakes, uranium mines
in northern Wisconsin, Illinois oil wells
anything to keep Mother from sitting alone
in the dark of our backyard at night
staring at smoky bonfires she built.
She took a job clerking at the IGA.
I left home for college, running away.

~ ~ ~

Around two in the morning he turns to me:
"It's eerie; tell your mother I said
it was eerie, double-E-R-I-E," as though
he's spent the last hours paging through
the dictionary of his life to find
a five-letter word meaning how it feels to die.
There is nothing I can do
so I crack the window just enough

to whistle the wind, a sound he likes for sleeping.
Sometime later he peels filmy eyes wide
and focuses far away to say, "I'm no longer
on the face of this earth.
What do you think about that?"
We're both surprised.
"Are you afraid?" I ask,
reaching out across the bridge
to wherever my father has paused.
"No, not afraid anymore," he tells me,
smiling, "It's all over."

THE ONLY CHILD LEFT

Two Women

Each day in the shower I run my soapy hands
over the scars on my belly and when I sweep
the dripping curtain aside, there she is, reaching
toward me. It's like opening night every morning and
I'm nineteen again, riding to the New London hospital

at 5:30 with Mr. Klingbeil who works at the plywood
factory and doesn't speak English.
At the hospital there's this woman who's had an
operation, something major, she always asks me
to change her sanitary napkins even though

she's well enough to handle that herself. Mostly
I worry that I'll have to feed the stroke patients
or that I'll be caught in the bathroom where I hide
when their trays come up early on the dumbwaiter.
This woman wears some kind of savage red nail polish

and it's flaking. When she grips my hand, I can't get
away. "You're so young," she says, as if it's something
I can help. Her mascara's always smeared.
I can't stand the helpless pleas in the eyes
of the stroke patients, the way they dribble

down their chins and have to wear bibs.
And this woman, how am I to know
that almost thirty years later I'll still wish
she'd check out. Black satin bathrobe,
pink mules — the kind with feathers but they're

scuffed and moulting — she's trying hard, believe me
but it's a losing game. How much of this is real,
how much of it I've invented, I don't know anymore.
Three years ago I almost died. It was the only time
I ever saw my doctor cry, standing by my bed

in Intensive Care he smoothed back my hair
and had to look away. That woman who haunts me,
sometimes she's in my mirror. I can smell her cheap
perfume. And she won't disappear. I'm just kidding,
there's really no resemblance. Not even in her laugh.

Thaw

This is white the color of asthma;
an exhalation of fog suffocates
the landscape with a sinister whisper.
January pauses, a deep sigh. Dirty

drifts windswept with dust
curve back into themselves
with lewd grace. Salt crystals,
traces of the last storm,

dull and cloudy jewels entice
from the edge of plow-scraped blacktop
where dog shit and crimped beer cans
are defrosting. In the cornfield

furrows reveal melting mounds, snow-filled
valleys, muddy graves. Elbows
of broken stalks jut raggedly into
the phlegm like brittle yellow

bones. Out on the lake an ice fisherman
blindly slides a sled, stops to shift
a giant corkscrew over his shoulder
and dissolves—blaze orange to orange sherbet

to winter's baited breath — in search
of perch and bluegills and other splashing
life beneath the surface
of this bleached acquiescence.

Souvenirs

This morning I found a white undershirt
that belonged to an old lover.
It is soft and worn thin with a slight
grease stain still on the left side
from the day he had to fix his bike,
the day he pulled the shirt over his head

and tossed it to me. It smelled
of his sweat and cologne and I slept in it
for weeks before it was thrown in the wash.
Now it clings to my breasts like old silk,
like the palms of my lover's hands when
they caressed me years ago. Once in awhile

I'll look down and everything I'm wearing
has belonged to someone else:
another husband's khaki shorts,
my mother's nightgown, my son's faded jeans;
it's almost as close as you can get,
like being inside their skin.

Every few years on the anniversary
of his arrest, the press reviews
a local graverobber's sordid tale;
how he'd unearth warm corpses
and take them home where he'd stitch
shirts and leggings, recycled

items of clothing from human skin.
I'd imagine him squeezing into women's bodies
and shuffling around his dim house
after dark, speaking in falsetto,
smiling as he sipped a cup of milky tea.
I saved all the newspaper clippings,

fascinated with the ghoulish details
just as I was intrigued with my baby teeth
I'd saved in a silver jewelry box:
nestled in the warm curl of my palm
they'd click together like ragged pearls
and I'd recall the trauma of pulling them;

each had its own tale, its own tenuous
thread. Mother threw the teeth out one day,
the clippings too, as though she could snug
the little teeth back in their bloody sockets,
pretend my smile was the same;
that nothing had changed.

Out of Breath, Out of Time

The linen inventory will be held
at one o'clock today,
a soft electric voice
murmers in the hallway

rushing haunted spectres in
to tally sheets and towels,
hushed mumbles in my fog.
Waylaid in early winter

I shall doze in hospital beds
days and nights toward another December,
dazzled by bright lights
then silence and searing pain,

anxious arms tugging.
I can hear my name,
unable to respond, and
shuffling feet passing

in the distance beyond my door,
the eternal nocturnal slippered
parade of patients pushing
IV poles, leaning on partners,

belching songs, farting
the music of their march.
Days ago: cloudlike gray poisons
settle into corners

of my curled body while
I fumble, find my way to Grandma's
wicker rocker mumbling mantras,
nursery songs of childhood,

songs to keep me safe, songs
I sang to comfort babies. Inside
my bowels fire blisters.
I cradle hot water bottles

until something breaks: the rage
I've been holding back in the dam
of my belly breaks forth so hot,
so hot I cannot keep it in anymore.

Blood pressure wafts
like ashes drifting down
gently in the shadowy nether
reaches. I sweep

through the elevator door
just as it is closing,
descending, black out, come
to just in time heart pounds

trembles, sweat wells
behind my knees dripping
wet all over. Just in time
this time slick with cold

and slippery I skid away
snagged sharp in the belly
and emptied but too fast,
too fast. Small gasps.

Pain better now I sip
ice, feel warm feel glowing
feel soothing voices above
around, moving down at me.

A nurse mumbles she is scared.
Don't be frightened, I tell her
and try to smile, floating
now. You should be, she

whispers strange honesty.
I'd had twelve hours
to live, they said
this morning

high above the snowflocked
city. The white nun pauses
in the door, the angel of
sleep and ultimate serenity.

She hovers over my head
blooming deep within my brain
while I wait, mouth open,
exhalation held so long

there are small breaths
between breaths and
I must stay alive to know
if I die before I wake.

Marian's Zucchini Bread

Zucchini slips from the silvery grooves
of my grater into a watery heap, then
I slide it, 2 cups green and dripping
toward a measuring cup, press it down.
Bountiful zucchini, still sleek and fat
after the rest of the garden has succumbed
to frost. 3 eggs, 2 cups sugar. Every time

I bake this bread I think of you, the recipe
in your handwriting, purple ink now smeared
and splotched, the corner torn — a remnant
of those days I needed friendship, macaroni
and cheese in your student apartment.
That was long before your babies,
before our mornings of modern dance, night
classes in life drawing; before
the year we both were sick then
toasted our survival. In a drawing

you gave me years ago, a nude woman
hugs one knee, half her face washed in red
as she glances at a foot curled
beneath her. She could be crying blood.
Tears stain this recipe I'm following
and I feel guilty making plans for my own
life while you're still struggling;
your cancer wasn't caught; it keeps on growing.
When we met for lunch last year you wanted
to know if this was God's punishment, had you
done something to make Him mad.
Don't be silly, I said, gripping your hand.
I told you I was baking your bread

and thinking of you when I called the hospital
this morning but that was only partly true;
I hadn't been in the garden for weeks,
surely the zucchini would be shriveled.
What I meant to tell you was I'm sorry
I've been avoiding you and your pain,
the anguish you must feel, but
I couldn't, and I lied. So here I am
with slivers of zucchini stuck to my elbow,
butter on my hands greasing pans for the oven.
"That sounds wonderful," you answered
hungry for real home-cooked food again.
We'll celebrate survival again tomorrow,
share a sweet loaf flecked with green.

Catalin Valentin's Lamb

I shake my head and turn the page...
Catalin Valentin and her lamb
in the Peruvian mountains,
the flock of sheep, the cornfield

might all be part of an artful pose
and even if it's not, the photograph
invades her privacy and cheapens it.
Where is the leering boy behind the tree,

the outraged herdsman, the sickly ewe?
Nowhere in this image;
nor a hint of the woman's face under
the wide straw brim of her hat,

and then it doesn't matter.
I would have missed her without the red
sweater against the trees. My driver
pulls over, parks the truck and says

"Some women just like to do that."
I try not to get her crooked smile,
the missing tooth, and hope her sinewy
fingers won't give away her age.

So I've chosen a shot where she's looking
away. I can almost feel the downy curls
of the soft white fleece in my hand which cradles
the sleeping lamb on her lap and nothing

matters, Lamb, not the curious woman
and her camera, not the cocky guide.
You were hungry and nuzzled my dress
before I could undo my buttons.

Then I offered my breast and felt
the familiar surge of milk coming in.
Your frenzied wriggling slowed as you
suckled and snuggled at my side; I love

the kiss of your sweet mouth,
the eager pull of your soft gums;
the tug of your greedy tongue wrapped
around my nipple. Nothing matters,

milk is milk. Your eyes close
in contentment now. One last forgotten
dribble forms a trace of bubbles
along your velvet chin.

Saturday Night/Sunday Morning

A nervous terrorist nuzzled my neck
with the cold gray barrel of his revolver
Saturday night. He shoved it through
the open window of my dream,
asked if I was happy, then
called me a lying bitch when he let me go,

let me drive across a bridge still under
construction where I found an old man
without a shirt, with a purple scar
on his right arm who gave me directions
holding a turquoise plastic mirror
stolen from my mother's dressing table.

All I want, I sighed when he kissed my mother,
is to go home. The next morning she called
to ask me if we had pull-down steps
to our attic, was my husband happy
or sullen and withdrawn,
could I find *The Power of Positive Thinking.*

Yes and yes, I told her, yes.
I wanted to say, when I gripped
the wheel of my milk-delivery van
with bloodless knuckles in my dream last night
I announced that if I'd die at the hands
of terrorists at least I would not be consumed

by crippling arthritis. I don't know
what that part meant, either. Well,
this morning six whistling swans
are gliding past in ruffled water
between the rim of ice on the lake
and the new lilac bush that branches

out of the frozen rock garden, a gift
to my husband on our last anniversary.
My third marriage. In fact, the third lilac
I've planted without staying anywhere
long enough to enjoy the promised
blossoms. When I was a child

and homesick my father would rescue me
and never got angry. I'll keep looking —
somewhere there'll be a light in the kitchen,
a soft bed in sweet darkness and someone
who'll say everything's all right now,
everything's all right. Don't be afraid.

Killing Frost

I awaken to gunshots in bleached dawn,
begin each new day on a note of death.
Duck season. Hunters hide in the marsh.
Saturday we canoed the Yahara, slipping between
painted decoys that bobbed on our ripples
and in the reeds men in camouflage cradled
guns and watched. I have felt these birds fly
across the ceiling of my study and when I look up
they have vanished. I can only see their shadows.

Tonight we shrugged further into our jackets
and went into the stillness to cover the tomatoes,
peppers, carry pots of geraniums inside.
The sky was deep and crystalline — no wind,
sharp stars. Red Mars stared out of the east
with its bold eye. We'll salvage what we can
from the threats we watch and wait for, things
lurking on the edges of my peripheral vision,
this feeling of unyielding change.

Tomorrow every blade of grass and fallen leaf
will be muted by a soft veil of icy white
gentling the damaged landscape. Even the raccoon
lying dead along the road will be frosted,
luminous. The cat stretches,
sighs, curls closer to my thigh. In this dark night
winter moves stealthily over the countryside,
a V of geese on its leading edge, pulling it
closer, over the Canadian border.

Sonnet for Jay

The wedding was not the wedding of my dreams,
your father's folks, my family, that was all...
The minister's shirt was frayed and no one sang,
no organ rejoiced. That night a spring rain fell.

My dress was silk but borrowed. I trembled with fear
knowing everyone there was aware of my secret shame.
You'd be born in autumn of that year,
in summer I turned twenty-one. My mother came

to diaper and bathe you, as if they all forgave
the hurt I'd caused. My only son,
I've waited in dread until now for you to say
the angry words I hoped would never come.

Please understand: we loved each other then.
Don't make me pay again for what might have been.

The Woman Named Yesterday
Is Playing With Dolls

Under the lilacs in an untamed corner
of Great Aunt Jenny's garden she's singing
a mother is all she has ever wanted to be.
How I love you, Little Sara, I would die
for you in a moment without a thought.

The strongest love she'll ever know,
this motherlove knit up of blood.
When her babies are there her house
is alive, the air splendid with laughter
and music they invent. She gives them

cookies and makebelieve after school,
reaches toward sweet faces to feel
the touch of warm flesh on flesh
but cannot say "How I love you,"
and when she pulls back to see

her son and daughter standing free, she
is aware this pulling apart will be forever
someday. When it is, when
no one is left behind to play
in the hideout they shared among scrub oaks

clustered near the fenceline, she
turns her back to the wind's soothing sweep,
hugs rough bark, feels it shudder,
and branches of tight buds like little
clenched fists waiting to explode.

~ ~ ~

Her husband kneads her breasts in bed
as though they will rise in the warmth
between the sheets and need punching down. She knows
her despair worries him. Sex is their cure-all,

has been since college, before she got pregnant.
Her wet eyes recall fumbled groping beneath
an army blanket in the Studebaker's back seat,
a policeman's probing questions while she sat 55

in a squad car, jeans still unzipped. Now
he says with marriage he has a right
to take her on the kitchen floor and when
she pretends to be asleep hears him mutter

in the shower, pulling at his hot, wet body
with soapy hands, punishing lashes of his towel:
"Fucking Bitch, Stupid Cunt!" One day without him
for the first time in a long time

she realizes her escape in a quick dissolve.
A subtle bit of whimsy crawls
across a waiting room wall; she traps it
in her palm, holds it tight and turns it over,

explores the struggling stubs of its legs,
prices of tickets to anywhere, letting
it wiggle, feeling its shallow breath
the thud of its tender heart racing.

~ ~ ~

He doesn't care. Or if he does he doesn't
know how to show it, but she thinks he'd rather
avoid having to care and maybe being alone
will be worse except she'll be free to turn

off the lights whenever she pleases and leave
her shoes on the floor, squeeze the toothpaste
fat in the middle again. No assurance
of quality in a future like that and a kiss

isn't enough to heal major surgery. So, when
did the break occur, he wants to know
but it was all a matter of time and time
usually wins. This time she'll gamble on the come.

~ ~ ~

Missing in Action seemed appropriate. She wore
a bracelet for a prisoner of war that year,
a soldier who'd disappeared in Cambodia. But it tore
her wrist the first time she went to bed with another man

and never put it on again. Now she sits
on her porch roof, late summer, baggy pants
sponging dampness from an old woven chair.
Trying to resist peeling paint with bare feet

she rocks and considers Kierkegaard, the results
of her adventures with a lingering anxiety
tenuous to her touch, transparent as blue
veins and cold as sharp metal circling her arm.

She tells her lover she has panic
attacks and hyperventilates at stoplights.
He drives her to the market, shows her
back streets, clues to find her way

in oblique angles. They are never more
than lovers, often less but he is kind.
Fragile flowers tremble, flutter in the cup
of jasmine tea she hands him with her poems.

Bob Dylan's his favorite. And when he writes
to say goodbye the summer's almost over.
She lost control of her life somewhere;
her son is sprouting acne and pubic hair,

her baby girl buys 45's of rock singers
she's never heard before. Voices flutey
as harmonica chords float through the backyard
neighborhood, each house a separate key.

~ ~ ~

The Arboretum is lovely in May,
they hurry to reach the lilacs before
the rain. Gray clouds creep overhead
and already a fine mist wisps the shadows

mingling perfumes of purple blooms,
magenta, blue and rose. Her daughter
leads the way, pausing to savor
the fragrance of each variety and they smile,

sharing the palest blooms that always
seem the sweetest. But it is a pale day

despite their warm laughter. She watches
the young woman hurry through wet grass

from lilac to lilac, her best friend now,
this woman the age she was when she gave birth
and suddenly she wants all the years
back again, she would give anything

to be twenty, to have both of her babies
in her arms, the songs of whippoorwills
on the prairie, birdsfoot violets in the sand.
The mourning doves, and even the delusions.

~ ~ ~

Smoke alarms of smoldering garbage, wood smoke,
burning leaves wake her in darkness: their house
is on fire. She knows she can still carry
one of her children over each shoulder;
every night weighing their limp bodies

sleeping over her arms as she finds her way
downstairs, three sad stories of dreamsmoke
to safety. In this she is secure, she will
always save them first no matter where she is
or how unbalanced her steps have become.

She wants to tell them they have
given her life its most profound pleasure;
she wants them to know how hungrily she waits
to be with them, the need rooted
and physical as desire,

without that dangerous edge.
At midnight, bumps and rumbles
her mother's ear is still attuned to
signal warnings even though
the odd slur of wind around the eaves

may only be the innocence of night,
a deep chill thumping timbers.
It's just the cold, she whispers to the only child left,
the one she carries within herself,
the child with the name she's always answered to.

Just the cold tumbling down below zero,
you're not alone, I'll always be right here.

IN THE SHADOWS OF THE FOOTHILLS

Seven Steps to a Song and Dance

Experience isn't interesting
till it begins to repeat itself
in fact, till it does that,
it hardly is experience.
Elizabeth Bowen
The Death of the Heart

My son saw Bishop Tutu jogging on Kendall Avenue last week,
past the house where we lived after I left his father.
I want to use that in a poem but don't know how;
and the fact that sometimes I suspect my life is just
a case of mistaken identity, that's been on my desk
for awhile, too. Today I received a letter from a therapist

listing a new workshop, *Making the Heart Connection.*
One afternoon I spilled my sorrows into his lap by mistake
and when I turned toward the door he took me in his arms
to say I qualified for one of his famous hugs. But I was
afraid I'd feel an erection if I let him hold me close
and when we met a year later at a party I tried to hide.

Yesterday I was in the copy shop and a woman next to me
was snipping outlines of her bare feet from xeroxed pages,
then coloring the letters written inside them with
magic markers. "Foot Massage Classes," the footprints
announced. I recalled the time Swami Ajaya took my feet
and placed them in his lap in the darkened basement

of a small town motel and said, "Your feet will blossom
like flowers." And they did, after I relaxed
and let him touch me in such an intimate way.
I was married to my first husband then. He was there
Friday when we had lunch with our children and our son
told us about Bishop Tutu. "Didn't you give him a high five,"

he asked, reaching for another slice of pizza; we were
such a happy family, laughing in all the right places.
My daughter assures me even the sad times are grist

for my life story because I seem to carom from one strange
encounter to another. Nevertheless I turn away and refuse
to meet my own glance reflected in the poor light

in the department store fitting room, scars on my belly,
traces of real pain. I never see myself from those angles
in real life. I auditioned for this role one June morning
before the full-length beveled mirror that's followed me
all the way to this new house and told myself I must always
remember what I look like now that I am four years old.

Flag Day

I had the feeling I was in one of those
endless on-the-road films, heat like a furnace
on the Illinois prairie and our little red
car with no air conditioning, one-hundred-seven

degrees that day. Most of the way
too hot to talk and you had the runs
at Lincoln's tomb where we posed for dumb
tourist snapshots, stood as far away

as we could to make each other tiny,
got ice cream and milkshakes in one little town
and a beer at a dark and crummy fisherman's bar
in New Boston along the shore

of the Mississippi where I had to pee but
didn't know for sure which door, "Inboards"
or "Outboards," and pushed the wrong one
then blushed in the mirror after I got inside.

Coming into Oquawka we saw the sign:
Visit the Grave of Norma Jean (Elephant).
And on the granite monument by the watertower
we read about gaunt Possom Red Evans

and the circus' only elephant struck
by lightning there where she was buried,
Possum's pliers and the tent Norma'd raised
still undisturbed in the yellowed clipping

set in a frame with some old dried flowers.
Late afternoon we followed a truckload
of Iowa pigs so many miles that when
we pulled into Keokuk the ventilating

system of our Chevrolet was stinking, sour
with pig piss but the motel had a pool
and after the TV weatherchannel assured us
the windchill was only one-hundred-and-two

we floated there lukewarm and weary. I saw a man
watching me from the window frame of
in an old brick building across the street
four floors up, sleeveless undershirt,

tattoo on his bicep. My God it was hot.
I set my Seven-up on the side of the pool
and swam around on my back a little while
longer just to give him something to look at.

Definitions

A woman who looks like me sat on the shore
across the lake and watched our house. She
saw you walk onto the grass to light the grill.
She could see the flash of flame as you

touched match to charcoal. Over the sunset stain
that reddened the water she sent this message:
please wonder where I've gone.
Every seven years the cells within our bodies

recycle; function, die and are renewed. Seven
years before her Tarot cards revealed her
disillusionment. The next day she wrote
"I must guard against giving my secret needs away,"

pretending self-reliance wearied her; she yearned
to curl in someone's lap and be comforted.
She is still seduced by kindness and wistful dreams.
Early this winter she was driving behind

a battered pickup on a country road. She saw
white puffs of down suspended in the air
like hesitant snowflakes and as she drew closer
a giant white wing arched out over the right fender,

fluttered, then disappeared. Bits of down floated
onto the shoulder. The wing stretched and flapped
again, in distress. She knew what must have been
captured but did not want to know for sure

and decided there was an angel bound and gagged
in the back of the truck. Things are
usually so much less than she desires,
so much less than she intends.

Cur

He awakens when I do, just before sunrise
and when I open my eyes the same old doubts
nose up against me like the cold, wet snout
of this impatient mongrel who wants out
no matter how many times I brush him away
and there we are, you and I, pounding on each other
like that night you tracked dog shit all the way
upstairs, then rinsed your shoes
in the kitchen sink, turned out the lights
and went to bed, leaving me to
scrape and scrub. I ♥ misery
has been painted on his water dish
for five years now and we feed him our excuses
three times a day. He needs to be
grabbed by the scruff of the neck more often,
shaken up while one of us hollers.
Don't let his wagging tail
fool you, I can hear his growl
of dissatisfaction just outside the door.
He wants to be let back in. Sooner or later
we're going to have to give him a name; he's
getting fat, taking over the house, dogging
our footsteps, chewing the edge off our smiles.

Walking the Dog

If I don't open my eyes I might be
anywhere else. Like Proust
I revisit rooms I've awakened in
and wish this would be England again,
the fragrance of just mown hay
sweeping through my window,

the leaded glass open to rolling fields
and in the bathroom a child's book
about castles that I'll finish while
soaking in a steaming tub. Last week
I sipped my coffee beneath pine trees
on the shore of a northwoods lake

listening to loons.
What frail magic is diffused
in morning mist to make my world
one of promise again
and again; the fragrance of tasseling
corn, of damp clover, pine.

I can feel the sun rising now
through the curtain and know today
will be hot. When I get up soon
to walk the dog there will be
a lemon haze at the edge of the woods
where tall weeds and grasses

beguile the path with invitations.
But this guest room futon is unforgiving
and I hear my husband turn to silence
the alarm next to his bed. After
a moment Bix bursts through my doorway
in tail-wagging delight, burrows

next to me: he prods his snout
beneath my elbow to tug at the pillow.
"Come back with your third husband,"
Mrs. Wright called when I left her B&B
for Devon that morning, headed out
the driveway of the old Sussex farm

and imagined myself married again.
I hear her hearty laugh even now as
she calls, "Third time's the charm!"
So I climb out of bed, call the dog
for his walk. The third time you strike out,
you go under even if you scream.

Heights We Can't Remember,
Fears We Know By Heart

How long before I lose sight of yesterday
when we stood above Chicago looking down
on FUCK YOU SEARS foot-printed in snow
103 floors below in a nameless park. I hope

I recall we made love the night before, holding
each other until sunrise, because we have
so little time left now that we're falling apart.
At 18 I saw the world from the Empire State Building

one night. I don't remember the boy I was with
or the constellations that beguiled us,
small town kids in New York City. I wrote to my folks,
"I'll never forget this as long as I live."

But I have. I spent today searching for that letter,
hoping it will reveal more details but I was
given to exclamations thirty years ago:
"It was really neat," is probably what I said.

I wrote a dreamletter to my high school classmates
last night asking if I could please
do the last thirty years over; they hadn't turned
out the way I'd planned. But my old friends

just gave me a knowing look and smiled,
middle-aged now, those kids who sat beside me
munching popcorn, watching *An Affair to Remember*
in the Manawa Theatre; the tragic scene where

Cary Grant waits for Deborah Kerr to meet him
at midnight, New Year's Eve on top of the World's
Tallest Building. He hears ambulances, police sirens
but doesn't look down, checks his watch, angry

that she hasn't turned up. "Everyone's looking at us,"
Betty whispered then, but I sobbed my heart out.
I wanted the lovers to have another chance.
I didn't give a fuck what anybody thought.

Rumblings

It's almost evening, still early
in your marriage. He has turned away
to hide in his music, play the piano
and repeat the same troubled measures.
You're ready to scream but take the car
to drive it off, flee to the country despite
the threat of heavy weather. You blame
your bad mood, not the warnings, although hidden
in the back of your mind are all the storms

you've ever known: the neon cross above
the Lutheran church down School Street flickering
pink against a black sky you eyed during Latin.
The afternoon the band ran for cover
you clutched your oboe, frozen to your chair
until a friend pulled you into the hall
crying as you crouched, head between knees
while trees ripped from their roots and crashed.
Now you avoid the rear-view mirror for miles

until you know you're lost, make a U-turn
at a deserted crossroads you've never seen
and wind hits your windshield.
Slammed by buffeting gusts you know you'll
end up in a ditch, tumble into a cornfield
and overturn, never see your children again.
You who have nightmares of twisting wreckage
remember *The Wizard of Oz* and follow
a foreign maze of rural roads curious onlookers

will assume you were blown to: like Dorothy
you're ready to go home. When the rain starts,
gray blankets slash in gusty shudders.
You pull off onto the shoulder

but you're afraid to stop. Up ahead two baby
funnels curl down from a thunderhead, twist
an erotic, deadly *pas de deux*, tuck up
again and disappear, You slow in fascination
staring long after they've gone. When you were

ten, tornadoes roared across the sultry summer
and in evenings you rode into the country
with Grandpa to view the damage. Orange sun
setting and sudden hush of twilight revealed
barbed wire fences strung with underwear,
farmhouse kitchens pared open, bricks
and shingles scattered in farmyards, dead cows,
unpaid bills: souvenirs of uprooted lives

the wind put on display. Now you find your way
back on rainwashed streets dodging fallen branches.
The garage door opens, swallows you, safe
at last so you go inside and there he's
still at the piano with the same old tune. This is
long before you know you will grow to hate his music
but you're beginning to see it all, stuck
in an endless refrain until you've memorized
every wrong note, anticipating the mistakes.

Calendar Girl

I learned about seduction at my home-town grocery:
bigger than life a blonde leaned forward
over the days and months of 1950,
bare shoulders draped with golden curls,

head tilted back. Her painted lips circled
a glistening tongue, a white smileful of teeth
and her merry blue eyes teased:
"Look what I have for you!" In each

palm of her manicured hands she offered up
a full, ripe breast like grapefruit,
rosy nipples bulging over the butcher's telephone.
Did I sound strange when Mother called

to add to the list she'd sent me for?
Did she wonder why I mumbled, blushing hot
while I feasted on my surprising
lesson in the art of arousal! Our first

time in the market together I recognized foreplay.
Fat strawberries spilled out of their wooden
boxes, cascades of grapes caught the light
like plump jewels. Plans made in aisles

for weekend meals, we stocked the cupboards
of your cottage so we wouldn't have to pause
when we were hungry. All along,
the day of the week we went shopping

for groceries was my favorite. Fridays
you'd come home cheerful, generous,
smelling of beer. I'd tear the list
from the refrigerator door, you'd sort

through coupons, we'd leash the dog
and drive to Tom's Market, park where Bix
could catch a glimpse of us as we'd round
each aisle. Milk and butter of course,

brown eggs, cream cheese, hot
peppers for chili, carrots for stew
and yeast for sourdough bread you'd bake
on Saturday. But lately

we've lost our appetites.
Our insatiable greed for each other
has diminished. When we go to the store
for the last time this spring

let's heap the cart with musky morels,
spears of asparagus and tart red rhubarb,
all that sensual stuff I still find myself
reaching for. We're beginning to push

our plates away and each other besides;
nothing works, not even sitting astride
your thighs, offering up my breasts
to your lips like luscious fruit.

Deep Purple

A pair of purple pajamas in this store window
is mesmerizing me; they're probably not my size
and the price tag is hidden. But I can see myself
wearing these pajamas on some vague, hazy terrace
I haven't even discovered yet. It's spring,

warmer than today, one of those weekends
you're so hungry for the sun you sit outside
with coffee, cinnamon toast and the Sunday *Times*
beside your chair. I don't know how or where
I earned this luxury of leisure and sunshine,

silk pajamas the shade of tulips I have loved,
or the reason for these dreams. This is
the time of year wild swans appear
on Lake Waubesa. I miss all my patterns
of seasons passing; I am turning my back

on whistling swans serene in open water
between thin ice and thawing shore
where tulips are beginning to stir: Purple Queen
of Night, Pink Emperor, Spring Pearl.
I've abandoned the swans along with the husk

of a woman who uncovers beds of roses,
trims winterkill and watches each day
for tulips planted one November afternoon
he turned the earth while I knelt
in the rock garden and ducks flocked overhead.

Woodsmoke was on the wind and a sharp edge
that smelled of snow. He brushed away leaves
with a gloved hand to dig cylindrical holes
and I dropped in bulbs white, smooth,
fat with promises. I glanced over

as he straightened up to stretch, smiling
down at me and my heart caught mid-beat,
I loved him so.
I wanted his promise to hold me tight,
hold me when ice crashed against rocks,

against silence of deep night, dark
so cold it cracked. But I smiled back
at him, smiled to myself, threw all the bulbs
together in a bag and chose at random,
gray clouds closing in, waves now rough

and harsh. We will outlast this winter
and many more, I thought, planting
one final tulip, packing the dirt tight
above. Now I stand in March drizzle,
nose against the plate glass window

like a hungry child, imagining silky
purple pajamas enveloping me in the midnight
gloss deep within the blossom,
the warmth of spring sun opening
the possibilities of improbable dreams.

I Find Myself Vanishing in the City

I must be nearly invisible now.
Here in the library to sidestep the wind
I greet an old man at the foot of the stairs
his face in a book. He does not respond
or even look up. "I've got it under control,"
you told me on the phone an hour ago. There's
a silvery blink of streetlights as I start

into the intersection and am nearly struck
by a passing car. At home you are
burning everything that bears a trace
of me or our marriage. I can imagine
your ritual pyromania on the floor
before the fireplace where we've made love.
Seated on the porch of our cabin we smile

at the camera until we go up in smoke
and settle, a sad lick of ash along with
Valentines, birthday cards, shards and shreds
of evidence caught in dissembling combustion.
Empty storewindows, dark reflections of wet
sidewalks shimmer, mirror my glance,
surprising the woman there. She has more fire

in her eyes than I remember in that photograph
you snapped in the Badlands, my hair whipped
aside by chill Dakota winds, striated moonscape
at my back layered in sallow, deathly shades.
Now the rocks begin to curl, turn black
and flick with flame.
My outstretched hand is charred;

my brown eyes blaze, refuse to disappear.

Dear Jack I'm in Wyoming

I'm surprised, after all these years
to look out my bedroom window and think of you
while I awake to the Big Horn Mountains
snow drifted down the north slopes

early morning sun sparkling on Cloud Peak.
After breakfast
I walk across the pasture
scuffing sagebrush, heavy dew,

and send a flock of wild turkeys scurrying
into the willow trees near Coal Creek.
I imagine you walking beside me
sizing up those quarter horses

grazing over there and shaking your head
at the lazy tending of this sagging wire fence.
I want to write and tell you
the Crow held these foothills

until the Shoshone and Arapaho moved west.
It seems strange to hear names and places
you used to repeat with reverence
when the West was your religion.

I'm wearing an old shirt of yours today,
a castoff you threw aside long ago
for one of our children. It's blue and faded
and soft as chamois now.

On Their Way West

"I am almost certain more
is expected of me than can
be had of one woman..."
Mary Richardson Walker
diary entry - 24 April 1838

A soft, oppressive stillness stirs my sleep
and brings me to this open window, straining
to hear any sound. No rustlings in the grass,
no leaves sifting from the cottonwoods.
And I know how it was, how the women

who passed by here felt this silence to their bones.
Beyond the trees the highway crosses
over Piney Creek on its way to the Big Horns;
a promise, once upon a time, or a dread
after months on the endless prairies

finally mountains ahead and a future
cut off from all we love. Along the trail
we have fought this fear as we've fought dysentery
and loneliness, endeavoring to be strong,
escorting each other back behind the wagons

to stand outward in a circle holding skirts
and fence a primitive shelter while the next
takes her turn. Our monthly dependence upon rags
pinned or tied into place like diapers
then washed and rinsed as privately as we can,

is the foremost of trials. And the law of the plains
demands that any of us still on our feet must serve
as nurse or midwife for those who are not.
We realize every day alive might be our last
and pray to love our husbands more, even though

they scold us and at times conclude that we are weak,
their tempers as short as piecrust. Oh, I confess
I sometimes despair and wish I had not married him,
but there is no retreating, meet it I must.
The thought often occurs, I am glad my friends

77

are not here to witness my sobbing and will never know
the state of my mind often resembles the weather
in time of thunder showers. I am desolate.
Nights like this a thick and liquid silence
like black ink splashes from the distant mountains

to foothills. We rise from our ground bedsteads,
from arms of men who see in only one direction,
brave the hauntings of our imaginations
and seek solace in this very moon, in these
stars whose small simmers are the only movement,

venture away from camp under this celestial stillness
with textbooks of astronomy to identify
the Big Dipper, Orion, Pleiades, anything
that will always be there for us,
anything that will always stay the same.

Artifacts

My body has become part of the landscape,
echoing the anatomy of mountains on the horizon
while I lie here in the grass observing
shoulder and arm, thigh and leg against

the red foothills we climbed yesterday,
hiking over the pasture, across Piney Creek and up
to the highest point where he tossed stones
into a rattlesnake den so I could hear their dry

chatter. Then, as a surprise, he
took me to a plateau that faced southeast,
an Indian ceremonial site, a cluster of teepee rings,
circles of bleached stones half-buried

in windblown dust and sage. He left me there,
left me to contemplate surrendering boots
sweater and jeans to lie in the center
of the largest ring, my head, arms and legs

a pentagram of spokes within the wheel of
magical rocks. Instead, I placed a chunk of quartz
in the middle — it had veins like rust — and made
a wish that came true last night.   He gave me

an Indian knife he found while camping in
the Big Horns, a flint thumbscraper flaked
to a fine and lethal edge. He knew
how I'd searched and tried to find one,

showed me how well it fit in my hand,
how to cut with it,
how sharp it was,
how easily it could draw my blood.

Porcupine With Magpie

At The Mint Bar in Sheridan you show me
how the wildcat's eyes light up yellow
every time the barmaid rings up a sale.
And you explain how the point count on antlers
of an elk or deer out here is only half

the number hunters use back home
where midwesterners have to brag.
On the jukebox the same song
you've played for me before, saying
it's from our era, your mother's

and mine, and I remember the night
you pulled me toward you, our bodies
fitting closely as we danced in that
dark and smoky roadhouse. I felt
as foolish then in my desire as now

and I ask you to decipher the brands
carved into the wall but I'm not even
listening, knowing only that you're touching
my arm and the smile I'll throw back at you
later when I read my poems or the easy laughter

we'll share while you drive me back
through the mountains will not come
from a wish to cradle you to my breast
like a son, or the funny name you'll give
to the dead animals in the middle of the road.

Dancing with a Cowboy

We waltz around in circles at Buzzy's roadhouse
welcoming the miserable mountain lion
who cowers in his lair above the beer cooler
next to the buffalo head, the antelope

and the Wyoming bumper sticker, *"where
men are men and the sheep are nervous."*
I watched a sheep herder ask Luann
to dance one day when no one else

was in the bar, when windows shook
in dusty wind and his pickup stood
at the gas pump out in front. Tonight
snow is on the way, why not celebrate

this half-starved, toothless trophy.
"Buzzy never would 'a shot the thing
if it'd been healthy," the cowboy shouts
in my ear. I barely feel his touch;

he holds me stiff-armed, shyly trying
not to move against me until someone's fist
drops a good ol' boy at our feet
where the pooltable usually stands.

"Paint Me Back in Wyoming," the jukebox wails
and I think about painting myself out here
forever instead of east of the Big Horns
where the steady glow of Jupiter

is rising now, closer to the earth
than it has been or will be for thirty years.
The cowboy says he'll buy me a beer. I could
fill those sharp-toed boots of Luann's,

zip her tight Lee jeans in the shadows
of these foothills, be a barmaid of mystery,
shake dice, shoot pool, have
my very own double-wide, a color TV

for the Rapid City station, a big old dog,
maybe a four-wheel-drive with a little
bit of gumption. You get six songs
for a dollar on the jukebox

here at Buzzy's.   You can waltz
with cowboys every night, you can
sing along with Patsy Cline. You can
lose your teeth, get lean, and smile.

Sara Lindsay Rath was born in Manawa,
Wisconsin and was educated at the
University of Wisconsin-Madison where
she earned a degree in English, and at
Vermont College of Norwich University in
Montpelier, Vermont where she received
an MFA in Writing. She is the author
of three previous books of poems,
including *Remembering The Wilderness,*
awarded The Banta Award in 1984
by the Wisconsin Library Association.
Currently residing in Menomonee Falls,
Sara has taught creative writing for the Univer-
sity of Wisconsin Extension and is currently on the
associate faculty at Goddard College, Plainfield,
Vermont.

Cover design by Jane Campbell
Cover art by Patti Genack